D1661026

THE LION IN ME

THE LION IN ME

ANDREW JORDAN NANCE ILLUSTRATED BY JIM DURK

PLUM BLOSSOM BOOKS

BERKELEY, CALIFORNIA

Plum Blossom Books, the children's imprint of Parallax Press, publishes books on mindfulness for young people and the grown-ups in their lives.

Parallax Press
P.O. Box 7355
Berkeley, California 94707
parallax.org

Cover and interior design
by Debbie Berne

Printed in the United States of America

Library of Congress Cataloging-in-Publication Data is available upon request.

1 2 3 4 5 / 23 22 21 20 19

For more information on how to tame your lion go to:
www.mindfulartssf.org.

MAY WE ALL LEARN HOW
TO TAME THE LION WITHIN.

I have a lion in me!
But it's not a lion I can see.

It starts in my stomach first.
It feels like I might burst!

When the lion starts to growl,
I want to give the biggest howl.

My fists start to clench and knot,
and my face gets really hot!

My body starts to tighten and tense,
and I lose all my common sense.

My heart starts to beat really fast.
I never know how long it will last.

When the lion takes over my mind,
I see red and am no longer kind.

I want to scratch things with my claws.
I want to tear things with my jaws.

I wish I knew the lion's name,
so I could grab it by its mane.

The lion can get so very wild,
acting like the meanest child!

I know when the lion rears its head:
when my family wants me out of bed.

Another time the lion gets in a huff?
If someone tries to take my stuff!

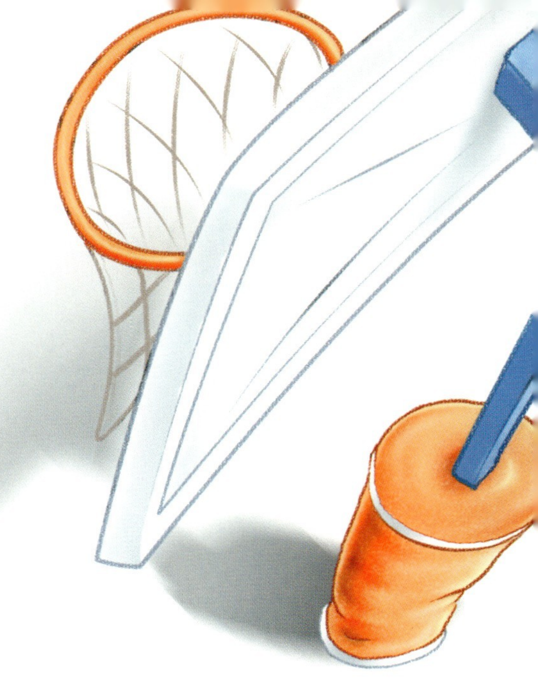

I think I know the lion's name.
It's **ANGER** that I have to tame.

When **ANGER** starts to growl and rage,
I try to breathe and say, "Behave!"

When I feel ANGER start to roar,
I take a deep breath and count to four.

ANGER can calm down that way,
getting tamer every day.

Some other tricks when **ANGER** shows its face:
I read my favorite book in a special place,

or speak to an adult, or take a walk,
which can make it easier to talk.

If I notice **ANGER** starting to attack,
I stop, I breathe, and it shrinks back.

ANGER just passes right through me.
I can tame it by naming it, and I feel free.